The Story of Grace

Evelyn Cape

Word of His Mouth Publishers
Mooresboro, NC

All Scripture quotations are taken from the **King James Version** of the Bible.

ISBN: 978-1-941039-11-3
Printed in the United States of America
©2020 Evelyn Cape

Word of His Mouth Publishers
Mooresboro, NC
www.wordofhismouth.com

Table of Contents

Introduction

I told my mother, Evelyn Cape, some time ago, that she should write the story of her and my father's life together. It is so interesting, and a story that only our Heavenly Father could have put together. My brother and I were so blessed to have the Christian parents we had.

You will be able to see in their life story how grace did much more abound. All I knew was a real, genuine man of God, Preacher, and Dad. I am so blessed to be able to say that with the background he had growing up. That just goes to show you what God can do for an old sinner like him.

I can truly say my daddy was not about preaching for money. I can remember times he would preach, and I would only have a pack of crackers and Nu-grape for a meal. He was an inspiration to me in many ways. It certainly has helped me since I have been pastoring to have a mentor like my dad.

My prayer is that this book will bless your heart like it has mine, just to see how far God can take you. Bless His Holy Name.

Burman Cape, Jr.

Chapter 1

Early Years of Evelyn Cape

I'm writing this book in memory of my loving husband, Burman Odell Cape, Sr. Also, I want to dedicate this book to my dear sons, Burman Jr. and David, and to my grandchildren and great-grandchildren that I love so much.

Several years ago, I wrote down things and thought someday I might write them in a book. I only had in mind for my family to read this book, but I thought someone else might like to read it and just see how the Lord worked in mine and Burman's life.

Burman has gone home to be with the Lord and left me by myself, so I find comfort to go back down memory lane and write. My purpose is for God's grace to be magnified to whomever might take time to read this. My desire is as the Psalmist said in **Psalm 71:17** *O God, thou has taught me from my youth; and hitherto have I declared thy wondrous works.* **18,** *Now also when I am old and grey headed, O God forsake me not; until I have showed thy strength unto this generation and thy power to every one that is to come.*

I know I have already been blessed with a long life, but I feel like life has been so short. I fear because I know I've failed to redeem my time as I should. My prayer is for God to help me to spend the rest of my life to bring glory to His name.

I grew up in the mountains of Ellijay, Georgia, and then you go eighteen miles up in the country to Diamond, Georgia. Our lifestyle was so simple. I know it will be hard for younger people to understand compared to the way life is now.

My daddy's name was Fletcher Garrett. My mother's name was Romie Weaver Garrett. I had three sisters, Pauline, who is six years older than me; Omelene was about three years older and died when she was around two months old of crib death. Bennie Mae was five years younger than me. I was the poor middle child. Some days I played in the playhouse with Bennie Mae, and then sometimes, I wanted to be like my older sister, Pauline. She was always smart and could do so many things I couldn't do. We were born and raised in a two-room house. One of these rooms was our kitchen and living room combined. We cooked, ate, and lived in this room. The other room was our bedroom with double-sized beds in one room. No one had a bedroom by themself. No one had electricity, water, or bathrooms in their house. We had oil lamps for our lights and a wood cookstove to do our cooking on. No fans or air conditioners; you can't believe how hot it was in the summer or how cold it was in the winter. I can remember water being frozen in the water buckets in the house where we lived.

We carried our water from a big spring. They had water buckets on the front porch on a shelf, wash pans to wash our hands, and a dipper in the water bucket for everyone to drink out of. I had a small bucket for me to carry water to fill up the big bucket. When it was time to do laundry, we had a big black wash pot close to our spring that they filled with water. Then we made a fire around it to heat water for the laundry. We had wash tubs on a bench and a rub board with a bar of Octagon soap. You sure needed a strong back for this job.

My daddy and mother made a living on a farm. We grew everything we ate. This was a lot of hard work with no pay, no fun, and no time to play. They had a job for everyone. We had a lot of the best vegetables around! Everything was better that was grown in the mountains. Along with the vegetables, the weeds grew well too, and the insects were very plentiful. I remember in the hottest part of the day they would send me to the gardens to kill the bugs on the green bean vines. This had to be done about every other day.

My mother worked so hard in the summer because she canned everything. Green beans, corn, tomatoes, pickles, beets, cucumbers, sweet potatoes, blackberries, peaches, kraut, pickled green beans, and apple jelly. Wow, she knew how to do it all and make it good!

It was always hard for us to have money to buy the things we needed that we didn't grow. We always carried our eggs to the store to exchange for the things we couldn't grow, and if the eggs were not enough, we would take a chicken fryer. They would take these eggs and chickens into the store's in Ellijay and sell them to the city people who didn't have chickens. Now one of the most exciting things in November was when it got cold enough to kill our hogs; it had to be cold enough so our meat would not spoil until it could be cured. We had a smokehouse where they salted it down and smoked the meat. This meat had to be canned because we had no refrigeration to keep it from spoiling.

Now, again, this was a hard job for my mother. She always canned sausage tenderloin and ribs and backbones; it was always so good. My mother just had the know-how to make it good. Our pork and chickens were all the meats we had unless daddy went deer hunting, then we would have deer meat. We always had a hot breakfast with biscuits, gravy, and sausage, ham, or tenderloin. If this meat was all gone it would be streaked meat. Sometimes we wouldn't have money to buy flour for biscuits, so we would have to eat cornbread for breakfast. No such thing as cereal in the mountains. We couldn't always have eggs because we had to save them to buy other things. Our drinks were always coffee, milk, or water; we never had Cokes. We also never had ice cream or bought cookies. A few times I remember having banana pudding. Our desserts were cakes, cobblers, or pies and they were peach or blackberry. A lot of times, there would be periods when we didn't have sugar or flour, and money was always scarce. Christmas was never any big deal at our house. We never got toys. We would get oranges and peppermint stick candy, and my mother always had a good dinner.

I can remember having two dolls growing up, but Santa Claus didn't bring them; my aunts bought them. For our paper dolls, we would cut pictures out of a Sears' catalog. There would be men, ladies, and children if we were lucky. We had a shoebox that would be our car to let our dolls ride in. We would play church with them. It was fun if you had never had store-bought paper dolls.

Let me tell you about our school. It was a one-room schoolhouse, and we had one teacher. She taught first through seventh grade. If you went to high school, you had to go to Ellijay. Not many kids ever went to high school. A lot of them didn't even finish seventh grade. We had no cafeteria. We took our lunch to school, and it consisted of a biscuit with sausage and sometimes an egg or jelly. At times I would have a baked sweet potato. We usually had a small little lard bucket for our lunch box. We lived about two and a half or three miles from school. We walked because no one had cars; EVERYONE walked. We would be so cold by the time we got to school. Our heat at the schoolhouse was only a wood heater.

When we came home from school there were always chores for us to do. We had to fill up the water buckets and fill up the wood boxes with stove wood. We had to feed the chickens, and this meant going to the barn and shucking and shelling the corn. Also, gathering the eggs, and, oh yes, I learned to milk the cows too. I thought I was being smart, but I found out it was no fun when it was a regular job for me to do.

We didn't come home from school bored because there was nothing to do; there was no such thing as that!

We were so poor that we didn't even have a radio. When World War II was going on, I would walk with my grandfather Garrett to a neighbor's house for him to hear the war news.

We thought these people were rich because they had a radio. The news reporter back then was Gabriel Heater. Of course, he's been dead for a long time now.

On Saturday, I would go with one of my aunts to a friend's house to spend the night just to listen to the Grand Ole Opry from Nashville, TN. That was a real treat!

Another treat we loved was our Grandfather and Grandmother Weaver, who lived in Canton, GA; they would drive up to see us. Grandpa had thirty-three grandchildren. He bought everyone a rubber ball, a real ball that would bounce. Can you imagine what the owner of the store thought about a man buying thirty-three rubber balls? All we had was a rag ball we pitched to each other. We had so much fun with these balls that would bounce.

My Grandma raised chickens, and they would bring us chicken feed sacks that had print designs. My mother then would make us chicken feed sack dresses. We dearly loved them. We thought they were the best!

Something else that was different in those days was when a lady was expecting a baby, she never saw a doctor until time for the baby to be born. The doctors came to the house, no such thing as a nurse; there would be a granny woman who would help the doctor. They would build a fire around the big black wash pot to have hot water. Several of the ladies died in those days giving birth to babies, mostly from infections, high blood pressure, etc. If the woman had a hard time giving birth to the baby, then it was sad because the doctors were not trained to help them like they do now. There was no such thing as anything for pain. I guess this is really natural childbirth!

When my sister, Bennie Mae, was born, I had no idea there was a baby coming to our house. They just didn't tell kids things like that. They sent me and my sister Pauline to our grandmother's house. When we came home, we had a big surprise, a baby in the bed with my mother. Now I always loved babies, but it took me some time to adjust to someone taking my place with my mother, but when I got over my jealous spell, I thought she was great, <u>and I still do</u>. I love both my sisters. We are BEST friends.

Chapter 2

Evelyn's Church Life Growing Up

I'd like to tell you now about our church life. My mother was saved at fourteen years old, and so she was a Christian for all of my life. My mother's parents were Primitive Baptist. My daddy was not a Christian until I was about seven years old. In fact, he was bad to drink and also to make moonshine whiskey. He was not a violent person and wasn't mean to us, but it still made things bad at our house because if he was drinking, my mother was sad and would sometimes cry. I remember this would always upset me. He said he made the whiskey to sell so we would have money, but it never worked out that way; we still didn't have any money. I remember when they were making whiskey that my sister and I would take his dinner to him up in the woods at the whiskey still.

The only church we went to was a Primitive Baptist (Calvinist all the way). They didn't believe in music, so they sang what they called four-note songs. Sometimes my grandmother Garrett would shout when they sang some of the songs. She was a Christian who enjoyed her salvation at home and church, too. I don't know how she survived in this kind of church!

I remember most of the ladies and men both either dipped snuff or chewed tobacco. On each end of the pew and in the middle, they had a wooden box about ten by twelve inches with sand in it. Guess what this was for? Well, if you dipped snuff or chewed tobacco then you would need a place to spit. Believe me, they used those boxes. There were also a lot of the men who didn't have the victory over the moonshine whiskey and apple brandy. They wouldn't get drunk, but they were called dram drinkers. Burman would always say that these dram drunkards were as much akin to a drunk as a pig was to a hog.

All of the churches in the mountains in those days only had service once a month, so you had a chance to visit other churches. Praise God, a miracle happened; there was a Missionary Church about two miles from where we lived that was closed down. A young preacher boy, Waldo Brookshire, opened this church and started having services. My family started going there some. Brother Brookshire got a young preacher to come for a revival named Rance Cain. This was a preacher filled with the Holy Spirit with a burden and zeal for lost souls. A revival broke out like you would not believe. I don't know how many got saved, but there were a lot. My daddy and sister, Pauline, and two of my aunts were in the number to get saved. You can't believe the change at our house. It changed from a house to a home. My daddy was out of the moonshine whiskey making and fell in love with his Bible. My mother was so happy. Brother Cain was a God-called preacher and soul winner. He never met anyone too high up in this world or too low in the gutter of sin that he wouldn't tell them about Jesus. Not long after this revival, Brother Brookshire left and moved away for some reason. They called Brother Cain to be the pastor of the church. I don't remember us going back to the Primitive Baptist except for the times they had decoration Sunday. On that day, they would preach out in the cemetery and decorate all the graves with flowers. My mother and daddy and grandparents, aunts and uncles are buried there. We still take flowers but don't attend the services.

In about two years, they called Brother Cain to Macedonia Baptist Church. At this point, my family changed churches and went to the church Brother Cain pastored. I was about eight years old when I attended church on this certain day. Brother Cain never preached a message that he didn't mention about being saved and that if you were not, you would go to Hell. He would visit our home and had dinner with us several times. Every time he came, he would pray and most of the time, my mother would sing. My grandmother would shout. Now all of this began to bother me, and I would be afraid to go to sleep at night. Remember, as I told you, my Dad was reading his Bible at home. He always read out loud, and he was always showing my mother something he had found in the Scriptures. They were always talking about Jesus coming back, and this was called the end of time. It was beginning to bother me a lot, but no one ever talked to kids about being saved and these churches would not have an altar call or invitation to sinners unless it was revival time. Something was telling me that my daddy and mother would not think I was old enough to be saved. This went on until after I was nine years old. It seemed like forever to me.

Now when revival time came, they would always dismiss school and march us down that dusty road for about one mile to the church service. They had day services. God had mercy on me and let Brother Cain know I was lost. He preached that day and made the altar call, and he came back to where I was. His question to a lost person was always, "How is it with your soul?" I knew if he thought I was old enough, it would be alright with my daddy. So down to the altar I went. I didn't know how to be saved, but I was crying so hard I don't remember anything I prayed, but God knew the desire of my heart.

After I had cried for a while, Brother Cain knelt down by me and ask me, "Who's Savior is He?"

Then with all my heart I said, "He's mine." As soon as I made that confession the Holy Spirit came into my heart, and I jumped up and down and shouted His praises.

The Holy Spirit just put me right on the Romans road, **Romans 10:10** *For with the heart man believeth unto righteousness: and with the mouth confession is made unto salvation.* Then verse eleven says, *For the scripture saith, whosoever believeth on him shall not be ashamed.*

I'll never forget how wonderful it was to have that burden of sin gone. Just to show you how a change takes place when you get saved, there was a lady who usually sat by me, and I didn't really like her. She would get happy and shout. I didn't like that before I got saved. When I got saved all that feeling was gone. I was hugging this lady. Old-time religion makes you love people.

Now, another wonderful day was the day I got baptized in the creek below the church. The sweet Holy Spirit flooded my soul and let me shout His praises again. I know everyone doesn't shout when they get saved, but what really matters is if you know you have trusted Jesus to save you. There was something else special about that day. I had never had a dress that my mother didn't make. She went to town and bought me a dress to be baptized in. Someone had a camera and made pictures, and I have one I'm so proud of. Now these churches were so different up in the mountains, as I have said, they only had services once a month. We didn't have Sunday school and didn't believe in eternal salvation. We thought you could be lost again if you didn't endure to the end. Nobody ever preached on prayer or had a Bible Study. We had no Wednesday night prayer meeting, but thank God, they did preach salvation. Most of the praying at church was by the preacher, although when I got saved, it was just born in my heart to pray. I would pray when I walked to school or to the post office. My favorite time was walking to my grandmother's house. My grandmother was an old-time Christian who enjoyed her salvation at home. She had three more boys, besides my daddy, that was lost. She always had a burden for them.

As time went on, it seemed like money got scarcer at our house. It was during World War II and there were no jobs in Ellijay. My daddy went to Akron, Ohio, and got a job. My older sister, Pauline was already married. This left my mother, me, and my younger sister up in the mountains by ourselves.

Chapter 3

Mother, My Sister, and Myself Alone

My mother was a brave woman who was not afraid of hard work. So, she and I planted our garden. A potato patch and a corn patch. At this time, my daddy did his plowing with a yoke of steers, or some might call them a yoke of oxen. While daddy was gone my mother and I plowed our garden with the yoke of steers.

Something else Bennie Mae and I would do was when we would run out of cornmeal, we would shuck and shell a bag of corn and put it on a sled. Then we would yoke up the steers and take it to grist Mill to get it ground into cornmeal. Mother would say, "Whatever you do, <u>don't</u> you dare try to ride on that sled." What do you think we did when we got out of sight of our house? You guessed it! We would ride on the sled. Thank God, we never got hurt.

Nobody at all had cars or trucks. Everyone walked wherever they went. Only one man at our church had a car, and probably only two men had pick-up trucks. It was nothing unusual for people to ride in wagons. We were too poor to have one, but my grandfather did. Sometimes we would get to ride in back of the pick-up truck. This was a real thrill. Oh, I've ridden in a wagon plenty of times.

We grew up so poor that I couldn't wait to get old enough to have a job and make some money that would be mine.

It was during World War II, and the schools up in the mountains could not get teachers. Everyone was getting jobs somewhere out of town. So, the mountain schools were desperate for teachers. If you had finished the seventh grade, then they would let you teach. I begged my mother to let me try and get a teaching job. I was fourteen years old but going on twenty-one.

I applied for the job, and they hired me. I was going to make about $50.00 a month. At first, I thought it was going to be great, but I didn't know anything about controlling children because I was one myself. By this time, I was bored with this. Really, I was so sick and tired of living in the mountains. I hated it. Actually, I prayed God would help me get out of this place.

I loved my mother and wanted to help her, but it was just hard work and no money and no fun at all. I could not handle the school teaching job, so I gave that job to my older sister.

My Dad had two old-maid sisters who were living in Dalton, Georgia. They were working in Chenille Bedspread Factories. I began begging my mother to let me go stay with them and get a job there. Finally, she promised to write my daddy in Ohio because at that time there were no phones to call him. I had to wait for a letter to come back. I prayed every day the answer would be "yes."

At last, we got the letter back with the answer. It was "yes" on several conditions. I had to <u>save some money out of</u> <u>every paycheck</u> and <u>absolutely no talking to boys</u> or <u>even thinking of</u>

<u>a boyfriend.</u> I can understand my daddy thinking this because I was only fourteen years old.

The day finally came to go with my aunts to Dalton. If you were going into Ellijay, you had to get a ride with the mailman. He would let you ride for fifty cents one-way, round trip for one dollar. The Thomas Bus Company had a bus that went to Dalton from Ellijay for about fifty cents. I was so excited! The city of Dalton, Georgia, looked like New York to me compared to Ellijay.

Monday morning, I was on the streets of Dalton looking for a job. You didn't need to have proof of your age. No one ever asked how old you were. You just had to have a Social Security Card. I found a job real soon. The U.S. Ten Cent store hired me. I was thrilled, only to get disappointed that my boss was like a U.S. Marine sergeant. She had no patience at all for me to learn the cash register, so about two days later, she let me go. This broke my heart, but I didn't let it stop me. My next job was at Stewart Bedspread Factory inspecting bedspreads, bathrobes, etc. It was big money, forty-three cents an hour. I was fine with this for about five or six weeks. Then I heard of Dalton Rug Company was paying fifty cents an hour, and it was near to where I lived. I applied for a job and they hired me. I liked this job best of all. I was sewing on a machine mending bath rugs.

My aunts and I divided the rent and groceries by three, and then it didn't take that much to live. I would buy material and take it home to my mother, and she would make my dresses. I had bought new shoes, handbags, and a new winter coat with fur on the collar. Lipstick, nail polish, and all these things I had wanted for so long. I had money in my purse besides what I was saving each week. I felt rich compared to the way life had been. My aunts and I would ride the city bus up Cleveland Highway to Grove Level Baptist Church on Sundays. This also was during World War II. They had good services everywhere then. We could ride the bus for ten cents and ask for a transfer to ride back home, all for a dime.

At last, I was happy with my job, but I missed my mother and home. But this was what I had wanted, money of my own. We would ride the bus and go home some weekends. It was good to go back home and have a good meal my mother had cooked. NO ONE could cook like her.

God called her home to be with Him at the age of forty-seven. She had cancer. The doctors didn't have the knowledge back then like they do now about cancer. I'll never forget her testimony and her shouting God's praises on her death bed. That will stay with me for the rest of my life.

Yes, I had hard times growing up, but it was for sure I know I had good parents. They loved us and took us to God's house where we heard about Jesus and got saved. I thank God they taught us responsibility. Life is not always going to be easy, so at a young age it was good to learn some responsibility because there will be some hard times when you get out on your own.

I'm not a Calvinist because I know God had a plan for my life. I've told you about my life until I was fourteen years old, and I now want to switch over and tell you about a very special person.

Chapter 4

A Special Man Named Burman

I want to tell you, as I know it, about my husband's life, Burman Cape, Sr. He lived to be ninety-one years old. WOW, thank you Lord! He was born March 27, 1920, into the home of Levi and Willie Mae Cape in Hinton, Georgia. It was just a small place near Jasper, Georgia. His life growing up was a lot different than mine. All the church background of the Cape family was Methodist. I remember Burman's mother, Willie, telling me they were saved at the Methodist church when they were both young.

His dad, Levi, was an educated man with a college degree. He had the talent to build things out of wood and was also a good mechanic.

Willie was a wonderful lady, very smart and not afraid of hard work. She was raised in an orphanage and never knew her parents. She only had one sister and she died at a very young age.

Sad to say, his daddy allowed alcohol to ruin his life. Levi's education and his talents were of no benefit to him or his family because he took no responsibility for the support of his family. Burman had three brothers, Quinton, Serber, and William L., and four sisters, Virginia, Maurine, and the other two died as babies.

His grandfather was Lee Cape, the U.S. Marshall of Pickens County. His grandmother was Alice Cape. The Cape house is still a beautiful place at Hinton, Georgia. The new owners call this the Butler-Cape House. They rent rooms out for overnight stays, and weddings take place there also. His grandfather, Lee, had five children in his family. There were three boys, Levi, Waldo, Hobart, and two girls, Cora and Madie. Burman's dad, Levi, and his mom, Willie, lived in a small three-room house real close to his grandparents on that property.

Burman's grandfather, Lee, was always raiding the moonshine whiskey stills. He had no respect of persons even if it was his children or anyone else when he would raid them. Levi, Burman's dad, had said if anyone bothered his whiskey he would kill them. Levi came home for dinner and found out his daddy, Lee, and his brother, Hobert, had poured out his whiskey. He went into a mad rage and got his gun. Burman, then a four-year-old boy, was by his side when he shot and killed his brother Hobert. He shot his daddy, Lee, in the leg. Burman said his mother grabbed him and his brother and ran into the woods and stayed for hours. They were scared to death. Levi left before he got arrested and dodged the law for several years.

One time when Burman was seven years old, his grandfather, Lee, was raiding moonshine stills. There were some of the moonshiners who teamed up on him, shot and killed him, and butchered his body. They were not satisfied with just killing him; they shot him several times, cut his head off and carried it a distance from his body, and it was several hours before they found his head. Burman said he remembered they opened the casket and had a sheet folded up over where his head was, and all you could see was one hand.

Then when Burman was a young teenager, his favorite uncle, Waldo, had problems with the sheriff and went to his house. He threatened him and when Waldo left his house the sheriff shot him in the back and killed him.

Earlier I stated that Burman's dad, Levi, had dodged the law for several years, so this left his mother to make it as best as she could with all six kids. She had no family of her own to help her. Remember, she was an orphan and never knew her parents. Then for some reason she moved away from Hinton, Georgia, to Dalton, Georgia, while the children were still small. She was a very smart lady and not afraid of work. This was during the depression days when jobs were very hard to find. This was also before welfare checks were thought about. She had to leave her kids a lot to do whatever kind of work she could find. She would clean houses for the rich people in Dalton. She would sit with sick people and wash and iron clothes, anything that she could do to make a dollar to feed her family. Burman said many times his grandmother Cape would get someone to drive her to Dalton, Georgia, to bring potatoes, beans, cornmeal, meat, or whatever she could to help feed them.

He also said his mother, Willie, a lot of times would divide the food out for them with nothing left for herself, then she would go pray for God to provide the next meal. She never got welfare like people do nowadays, but God helped her make it. Burman and his brothers and sisters never knew the love of a daddy; all they knew of him was bad. He never provided anything for them; he was always mean to his mother, always threatening to kill all of them. After several years the law finally arrested his dad for killing his brother. He did some time in prison, and Burman's grandmother finally sold some of their farmland to get him out of prison. This was only bad for his family because he was so mean to them.

Willie finally divorced him. He lived to be sixty-three years old and followed the same lifestyle until he died. A preacher visited him on his death bed, and he was supposed to have gotten right. Our prayers are that he did trust the Lord. It is so sad to see people waste their lives. In spite of the way Levi treated them growing up, Burman tried to help him different times and tried to talk to him about getting right with the Lord. We even let him come to our house and stay for a while. Burman told him there was absolutely no drinking at our house. Two different times he had to make him leave because he got drunk. He was just one of those people you couldn't help.

Chapter 5

Burman as a Teenager and Early Twenties

Now I hate to write this part of the story about Burman's life, but I thought it would let you see what God's grace did for him and how far in sin the devil takes people. But I'm told God's grace and mercy can still reach them, so this story has a happy ending.

Burman made the mistake of starting to drink to when he was a young teenager. Then it wasn't long until he was getting into trouble with the law. He ended up having to spend time in prison at a young age. Every chance he got he would escape only to add more time and trouble. He never talked about this part of his life to people, but he talked to me about it several times. He would be shot at during the times he escaped, and only God's mercy spared his life to get saved. Also, in between prison time, he spent some time in CC Camps, the Civilian Conservation Corps. This was something they had in the 1930's and 1940's when President Roosevelt was President of the United States. For young men the CC Camps was very good for them.

After that, he ended up back in trouble and in prison again until he was twenty-four years old. He was discharged out of prison July 3, 1944. Willie took him to the emergency room on July 4, 1944, because he was having a nervous breakdown from all the bad things in prison. It was so scary for him to tell the awful things that happened such as friends getting shot by prison guards and prisoners killing other prisoners.

A boy got stabbed one night just after the lights were turned off. He flipped out in the floor and bled to death, just a few feet from where Burman was. This really upset Burman. But after some medical treatment and being at home, he was able to look for a job in October of 1944.

If you remember, I was working at the Dalton Rug Company, and Burman's mother

Willie worked there. I thought she was a nice lady, but for some reason, I felt so intimidated by her. Something was telling me she didn't like me. But guess what? One day her son, Burman, came to see her at work and asked for a job. They hired him! Before he had been there two days, guess who was looking at me. Every time I looked up or left my workplace, his eyes were on me. Smiling and winking those baby blue eyes, my face I know would be red as blood because it would burn, and my heart did flip flops. I am writing this right now in a motel in Gainesville, Georgia (as I reference before, I made notes for years to be put in this book). We are in revival over here and when I was writing about him winking, I looked across the room at him, and he gave me a big smile and winked at me. So, he is still winking at me fifty-nine years later (I just had to write this!).

Never had I seen a guy so handsome. He was six-feet and one-inch tall, dark brown hair, baby blue eyes, beautiful white teeth, and always a big Ipana smile. It was no time until he was asking me to go out with him. It broke my heart to tell him I couldn't because my parents would not let me date anyone. I didn't tell him I wasn't old enough to date. Remember just fourteen years old going on twenty-one. You probably would have guessed me to be eighteen. I was one of those kids that looked older than I was.

Every day and every minute we had on break or lunch time, we were talking. I was living with my aunts which were old maids. If I wasn't at work, they would very much know <u>every minute</u> where I was. Then I began to tell them I was working overtime. Burman and I would walk to a little restaurant, get a Coke, and sit and talk. Every day we loved each other more. One day he told me he would go to church with me if my parents would let him. I finally got the nerve to ask my mother when I was home for the week and her answer was "NO" without thinking twice. She said it with a threat to make me come home.

Burman was already talking about wanting to marry me. He was walking me part of the way home from work one evening, and I said, "Burman, there is something you need to know about me."

He said, "What is that?"

I said, "I am only fourteen years old," real quick

He said, "I don't care; I want to marry you anyway."

There were some Christian people who worked where we did who tried to talk to me. Someone let me know about his drinking and that he had been in prison. When I asked him about it, he didn't deny anything but told me he was through with that kind of life. He didn't want to drink anymore since he had met me.

Guess what? I was stupid enough to believe him. That was 1944 and World War II was going on, and the news came that they were going to close the plant where we worked because they had to have the material for the war. We knew what that would mean. I would be going home to Ellijay to my parent's house, and we would not see each other anymore.

Chapter 6

Getting Married

This was at Christmas time, and for some silly reason, we got mad at each other, so I went home to Ellijay to my parents for Christmas. I was so miserable inside, but I didn't let anyone know. As I said before, I never heard anyone preach on prayer, but after I got saved there was a desire born in my heart to pray. My favorite place was when I would walk to my grandmother's house. I can remember so well walking to her house crying and praying every step for God to help me. If Burman was not for me then I needed Him to help me know what I was supposed to do.

So, I went back to work after Christmas and went into the plant. I didn't even turn my head or my eyes toward Burman, but here he came to me as soon as he could, telling me how sorry he was, and being so sweet again. My heart melted like a snowball in the fire. I took this as my answer, and I still believe it was the right answer. We worked all week until Friday, and everything was fine; we were still talking about getting married. You didn't need to have proof of your age in those days, no blood test or no waiting, just go to the courthouse. You could just buy a license and the Ordinary would marry you. I knew the only way I could get married was just to tell my parents after I did it. I knew this would break my mother's heart and that my daddy was going to be really mad at me. I loved my mother so much, and I loved my daddy too, but I was so afraid of him. I had never been a rebellious child, but I didn't like the whippings that my daddy gave and how well did he know how to give them.

I could not stand the thoughts of going home to Ellijay and never seeing Burman again when the plant did close down. So on Friday, January 5, 1945, we worked until lunch time, then Burman walked me up the street begging every step he took for us to get married that afternoon and not go back to work until Monday. So that's what we did. I was scared to death. The Ordinary married us and Burman bought the marriage certificate. He was so proud of it that he went and bought a frame, and it's hanging right now in his study. It brings joy to my heart to look at it. Anyway, after we got married, we went by the plant where my aunt that I lived with worked, and I introduced her to my husband. She just about fainted. She didn't know what to think! Then I went to my apartment and got my clothes and went to his mother's house with him. There we stayed with his mother whom I was so intimidated by. She was very nice to me, and I soon found out why I thought she acted strange. She knew what I didn't about her son, that he had a lot of improving to do to be ready for marriage. I know she was worried about us.

Burman sat down and wrote my mother and daddy a letter (if you can believe that?) telling them he had married their daughter. I can't imagine how they felt when they got this letter. I was on pins and needles worrying what in the world my poor mother would do. They had never heard of Burman Cape, yet when I did hear back from them, they were nice about it.

Late that afternoon after we got married, we went downtown to Dalton to a drug store that had sandwiches; we had a chicken salad sandwich for our first meal together. This was the first time I had ever eaten out. There weren't restaurants everywhere like there are now. You have to remember I was from the mountains of Ellijay. Every time I eat chicken salad, I always remember the first meal we had together.

Then about the next week we planned a trip to go see my parents and let them meet their new son-in-law. So, we had to ride the bus from Dalton to Ellijay, then get a ride with the mailman eighteen miles up into the mountains to Diamond, Georgia. Then we had to walk about two miles from the post office to where they lived. There was not a paved road anywhere up there. The roads had been frozen overnight and then thawed up. You can't believe how muddy it was. We've always laughed about it since Burman had his pant legs rolled up almost to his knees to keep from getting mud on them.

When we got almost to our house, I was scared to death. I dreaded to face my mother and daddy. Burman said, "What do you think your daddy will do?"

I said, "I don't know" but the way I knew my daddy, I knew what he would want to do, that was to cut him an old fashion hickory and give me a whipping. But they were really nice about it.

I remember my mother had a good hot meal cooked for us. Burman always loved everything she would cook. We grew a lot of cabbage and my mother could make sour kraut like nobody else could. She always had pickled green beans. She would have kraut in two big churns in the spring where the water was almost ice cold. This was our refrigeration. Burman thought those were the best ever.

After my parents were so nice to us, it sure relieved a lot of pressure for me. Then we went back to Dalton to the plant where we worked which had closed. Burman's mother and I found a job at another place hemming dish towels. Burman couldn't find a job. So, we heard they were hiring men in Oak Ridge, Tennessee, at the nuclear plant. We talked about it, and Burman decided to go up there and find a job and a place for us to live and we would move there. I stayed with his mother and worked. Burman got a job in Oak Ridge, and I thought I would be going soon. (This was all a bad mistake.) The first weekend he came home after getting a job, he was drunk. I had really believed him that he wouldn't drink any more. I thought my world had come to an end. I cried my eyes out. Guess what? He cried with me but my trouble had just begun. He promised never to do this again. He was going to take me and buy me something if I wouldn't cry.

When I found out how much money he had I was surprised. I was surprised and disappointed he didn't have enough to buy his bus ticket back to Oak Ridge. So, I had to buy it for him. He didn't like staying up there so that didn't last long. He came back home and found another job in Dalton. His drinking had just started, and his mother was on my side. This caused a problem; she would fuss at him a lot. So, we finally got an apartment and moved out. Now, I had done what my daddy said I had to do with my money. I had saved money out of every paycheck. I had <u>big money</u>, $125.00, and daddy had given me a heifer calf. I often teased Burman that he just married me for my money and heifer calf.

We moved out into an apartment of our own, but we didn't have enough money to buy furniture. My sister, Pauline, loaned us money to buy what we had to have. We only had two rooms. No one ever gave showers in those days. That was not heard of. My mother made us a set of sheets for our bed out of scrap material they had bought at the plant where my daddy worked. We bought three towels and two wash clothes. My mother made us two quilts. The tops of the quilts were what I had pieced out of scraps when I was growing up. We bought three plates, two cups and saucers, two forks, two teaspoons, two tablespoons, two knives, two or three bowls, two small pots, one cast iron skillet that I still have, and a biscuit pan that was a must if you lived with Burman Cape. He had to have biscuits and gravy every morning. Although I had never made a biscuit, I had watched my mother make them plenty of times. I had never really cooked myself that much. I was busy doing other things like milking the cows, feeding chickens, gathering eggs, or carrying in water.

While we lived at Mrs. Cape's house, I learned a lot from her; I would always watch her. I wanted to learn exactly how she cooked, because she was a very good cook and so was my mother. Poor Burman was used to all the good things his mother cooked that were just right. I wanted to please him, so I thought that if I learned from his mother that would be sure to be right. I would try and would mess up, then I would try again. Burman was not bad to fuss about my cooking because by this time he knew he had married a child. In those days you had to learn to cook because you sure didn't have money to go out and eat. They didn't have restaurants like they do now.

I remember so well, I had promised God before we married, I would try to get Burman to go to church, but I didn't follow through on my promise.

Brother Cain always preached against going to the things of the world after you were saved. I had never been to a movie theater. My daddy wouldn't let me go anywhere like that. The devil told me, "You don't have to answer to your daddy anymore." So, Burman took me to my first movie. I thought this was going to be great, but deep in my heart I could hear Brother Cain saying, "Do you want to be at the theater when Jesus comes back?" God wouldn't let me enjoy the things of the world. I didn't want Burman to make fun of me, so I would go to all the carnivals and the circus. When the Grand Ole Opry stars came to Dalton for personal appearance shows, we would go. That was Burman's favorite thing to do.

The one thing he would never do was take me around any of his drinking buddies. He also would never take a drink in my presence. I just saw the effects of it when he came home.

I remember once he hurt my feelings when he was on one of his big ones. I decided I'd had enough; I'd just leave. Now my mother and daddy had moved to Dalton. I liked the fact they were in Dalton, but did I ever make a mistake when I went home to momma and daddy. When my daddy got through telling me what he had to say, I made my mind up I would never try this again. We were taught marriage was a lifetime commitment. One thing I can say in all of Burman's drinking is that he never physically abused me. We got along well if he wasn't drinking, but inside I was a miserable human being.

I was pregnant and we were expecting our first baby. I hadn't been to church in about one year. God dealt with my heart every day; I was doing plenty of praying.

On April 12, 1946, an eight-pound twelve-ounce boy was born, and we named him Burman Odell Cape, Jr. Burman was so excited about having a son. He didn't drink at all for one month. We were so happy! I thought my problem was solved. Then he started all over again only worse. He was not a person to stay drunk and not work, so he would always work through the week but get drunk on weekends.

Chapter 7

Salvation That Makes a Home

There were several people who worked with him that were Christians that prayed for him. I know my mother prayed, although my parents didn't know about the drinking problem. If they came to our house and Burman was gone out drinking, I would make up something to tell them so they wouldn't know. You can see why I was miserable, and God was whipping me for all the lies I was telling.

On the Saturday night of August 31, 1946, he was on one of his big ones. Sunday morning he was so sick; he usually wanted tomato juice. He begged me to go get it for him. I said, "No, I don't care if you die; I'm not going." He got up and started to the store. He was so sick that he had to sit down on the way. He said sitting on the side of the road he told himself, "I'm quitting this." When he came back, he told me he had quit. I had heard that until I didn't want to hear it again.

Over two weeks had passed. He hadn't drunk at all, and we were going to a carnival and our neighbors were walking up the street in front of us. We knew they were going to church. We lived close to Morning Side Drive Baptist Church, and the church was in revival. Burman said we better slow down, we are going to catch up with our neighbors, and they will ask us to go to church, but instead they just stopped and waited on us. Sure enough, they invited us! This was about the middle of the week.

Saturday night of that week we had gone to my parent's house to spend the night. They were always so glad to see the baby, Burman Jr. He was five months old. I was helping my mother cook supper. Burman was sitting on the front porch, and he called to me. He said, "I know you want to spend the night with your parents, but if we go back home, we could go that revival." I couldn't believe what I was hearing.

My mother said, "If he will go to church, then go home with him." So that is what we did.

I will never forget going inside that church. That was the most beautiful singing I had ever heard. We sat on the very back row. It was plain to see God was dealing with Burman. Would you believe, because we were there, they decided to run that revival another week. We didn't go back on Sunday, but Monday evening Burman came home from work and said, "We are going back to church tonight." I was so happy; I knew that he was under conviction. Tuesday night we stayed home to do laundry. We didn't have many baby clothes, so we didn't have a washing machine and had to draw the water out of a well. Burman thought all of this was too hard for me. He was always good to help me. We had to scrub our clothes on a rub board. He would do his part.

Well, praise God for Wednesday. I got Burman, Jr. to sleep and got on my knees and ask God to forgive me because I knew I was saved. He came home from work and said, "We are going back to church tonight. God is going to save both of us."

I said to Burman, "When the baby went to sleep today, I prayed and asked God to forgive me." That broke his heart even more.

When we got to church, my sister Pauline and I sat down about middle of the church. Burman went to the front seat of the church. When the preacher got through preaching, he said, "Let us stand for the alter call." Burman didn't wait for the singing to start, he got up and went to the altar and got on his knees. I gave the baby to my sister and went to the altar with him. He was crying, begging God to save him. I remember our neighbor, Sister Boyd, ask him in a few minutes if he didn't feel better. He said "Lord, No." He put his head back down on the altar. He said, "God if you don't save me, I'm going to hell." About that time, he lifted his hands up saying, "Good bye, old world, good bye." I think half of the church was shouting. I didn't think Burman would ever get through shouting and testifying. He praised God on and on. He has always said God called him to preach that night.

We went home a happy couple that night. When we got home, he went and got a bottle of whiskey that he had hid and went to the back door and poured it out and broke the bottle. We had a Bible my sister had bought us. He got that Bible and read a while before he went to bed. From that night on he always read before going to bed.

He got up the next morning and started out walking to work. Some of the people who worked where he did came by and actually stopped for him to ride. So as soon as he got in the car, they asked, "What happened to you?"

He said, "I got saved last night." They could really see the difference in his face. They were all shouting by the time they got to work. These are some of the people who had been praying for him. He joined the church that same week for baptism. These churches always baptized in the creek back then. When Sunday came for the baptism, it had started raining, so they mentioned calling the baptism off. Burman said, "I'm going to get wet anyway, I want to have it today." So that's what they did. He shouted and praised God again when he got baptized.

Burman started out all the way with the Lord. They had cottage prayer meetings in homes in those days. He went to every service they had. We didn't have a car; a lot of people didn't back then. I'll never forget how the people helped us. Someone would always come by and pick us up if it was too far to walk. He testified, shouted, and praised God everywhere he went.

The plant where he worked even allowed them to have prayer meeting on their lunch time. They had one hour for lunch, and Burman was in charge of the prayer meetings. On every Tuesday they had the meetings, and Burman would testify and shout even at these meetings. There were quite a few Christians that worked at this plant.

Preachers would take him to fellowship meetings; they would always ask him to testify. Happy Valley Baptist Church in Dalton always had prayer meeting on Saturday night, and he would always go to that. He stayed busy at night going to services. What a difference at our house. *Our house at last had become a home.*

Chapter 8

Preaching Was His Life

A lot of the churches in those days were foot washing Baptists, some didn't believe eternal salvation, or they didn't believe in paying tithes. We certainly had a lot to learn.

Burman tried teaching Sunday school, leading singing, Sunday school superintendent, and he couldn't do any of it without preaching. He tried everything just to get away from preaching, but it just wouldn't work. He even decided to go to Detroit, Michigan, and get a job making big money. He looked for a place to live, and then I would come to where he was. He said he would find us a church in Detroit. While he was there, he even made a trip to Canada. Thank

God, He spoke to his heart and told him he better get back to Georgia and preach.

Finally, after all this he confessed his call to preach. I had grown up in the mountain churches, and I didn't know anything about real victory in the Lord. I just went along with whatever, and I sure didn't know anything about being a preacher's wife. I just tried to please Burman and go along for the ride. Real soon after he had confessed his call to preach, part-time churches started calling him for their pastor. I know he was pastor of three of these churches at the same time. By this time, somehow, we had managed to buy our first car, a 1935 Ford. We were both so excited that we had a car. We were both working and made about twenty-five dollars a week each. We had to pay a babysitter for Burman, Jr. During this time my mother was dying of cancer. My sister and I had to take weeks about staying at my parents' house to help take care of her. I was only getting to work every other week.

I was pregnant again, and this time we lost our baby girl.

Then we had a funeral bill, hospital bill, and doctor bill, and we were borrowing money from one loan office to pay the other loan office. Have you heard of robbing Peter to pay Paul? That's what we were doing. Three weeks after our baby girl was buried, my mother passed away.

Our car would break down, and it seemed like it was every other week. A lot of the time these churches didn't even take up an offering. There were several people that were Christians where Burman worked, and they would help him more than some of these churches.

I'll never forget, one Sunday at a church, they took up an offering, and it was to be Burman's offering. Someone put a five-dollar bill in the offering, and the deacon went to count the money and held up the five-dollar bill and asked if someone put it in by mistake or if they wanted change back. It was worrying him for us to get all of that. The total offerings at this church would be between six to ten dollars. The pastor at Morning Side Drive had left, and they called Burman for the pastor. Remember this is where he got saved. They usually gave him in the twenties of dollars. This was the best part-time church he pastored. We always had a packed house and a lot of people were saved. They were also filled with tradition that was not backed up by the Word of God.

When I speak of tradition, I was raised that way. They didn't believe in a preacher studying and using any kind of books or help. They thought you just take a thought from some verse, and God then would fill your mouth. Some believed eternal salvation, others didn't. They believed a pastor should work on a job just like everyone else. They didn't believe in any kind of mission work.

In spite of all this, God wonderfully blessed his ministry at Morning Side Drive. As I said, we always had a packed house and a lot of people saved.

God was sending us to school and trying to teach us to pay our tithes. Burman had read enough Bible to know it was the right thing to do.

In the meantime, Burman had gone back to Hinton, Georgia, where he had lived as a small kid. He went to ask permission if he could run a revival in the Methodist Arbor. They gave him the okay, and God was surely in him doing this. There were over fifty people saved. Drunks, boot-leggers, and all kinds of lost people attended this meeting. They packed the place out for two weeks. Out of this revival, the Hinton Baptist Church was organized, it was in the schoolhouse where Burman went to school as a child. He was their pastor for about two years, having services the second and fourth Sunday afternoon at 2:00 pm.

We would have service at Morning Side Drive on Sunday morning, then drive to Hinton for Sunday afternoon, it was about fifty miles. Then we would drive back for Sunday night service at Morning Side Drive. Burman was full of zeal and a lot of get up and go in those days. These people built a small building sometime after we left. There were some good people there, but they were so set in their ways and traditions. There were so many lost people there. It was very difficult because if you tried to talk and help lost people, they thought you would deceive them.

Burman was young, and we still had so much to learn. When he pastored these part-time churches, he hadn't learned anything about premillennial doctrine, and they were all post millennial. Burman's education level was only the fourth or fifth grade. I get so much joy out of just knowing where God's grace and power brought him from. He had a zeal and desire to know and understand God's Word. **Psalms 37:4** *Delight thyself also in the Lord; and he shall give thee the desires of thine heart.*

Chapter 9

The Start of Full Time Churches

Then something wonderful happened. The Lord sent a preacher by the name of Lee Key to Dalton, Georgia; he did tent meetings, revivals, and street services. Most all the pastors of the part-time churches were afraid of his doctrine and advised Burman to stay away from him. But we did the opposite. We started going to hear him preach; he was a great soul winner. He had a burden for the lost and rightly divided the Word of God. He was God-sent into Burman's life to help him.

Brother Key advised Burman to get help in reading some books like the set of books of H. A. Ironside on the Bible. He also suggested M. R.

DeHaan. The Cruden's Concordance was the first book he bought. He was getting the Sword of the Lord. He would read these papers, so this was just the beginning of his buying books. Brother Key told him if you see a tract anywhere to pick it up and read it, and that there might be something in it to help you. He also would have Burman preach at his street services. You could have a crowd in most any town for a street service in those days.

A sad thing happened to Brother Key. He had been to visit a lost man and left this man's house and drove his car up on the railroad. He didn't see the train and was killed. This sure saddened a lot of people's hearts. He was a wonderful man of God. I know he will have a great reward for the people he helped. He sure helped Burman get what he needed to help him grow in the grace and knowledge of God.

Another wonderful thing happened when the Christian people who worked with Burman on the job bought him his first Scofield King James Reference Bible. He never forgot how happy he was about his new Bible. We have the list of all their names and how much each one gave. All of these dear people have gone on to be with the Lord. I still have the Bible.

God began to open doors of revival for Burman, and it was in the spring time that the first thing we knew he was booked up all summer. To do all this driving and work on a job was just more than he could do. God began to deal with him about giving up his job. That was another big step for us too. We had to buy a better car which was a 1942 Ford. His boss told him to just take a leave of absence. I was working at this time on a different job making more money than I had ever made, $50.00 a week. Burman and I both were proud of this job, but it was second shift. I wouldn't be able to go with him until Saturday nights. This would mean he would have to take Burman, Jr. with him a lot of the time.

He was preaching a revival close to LaFayette, Georgia, and was having a great meeting. People were being saved, and it was just a good church revival. A pastor and some of his members from Mount Olive Baptist Church in Rossville, Georgia, came to the meeting to hear him. They booked a meeting for him to come to Mt. Olive Church for a revival. This was a great meeting with souls saved. The meeting lasted two weeks. The pastor was an older man. But not long after this meeting he left the church, so they were in need of a pastor. This was a full-time church. The deacons came to talk to Burman about being their pastor. He had prayed about being an evangelist, but when this was offered to him it became a battle for him in his soul. We would have to move from Dalton, Georgia, to Rossville, Georgia. I would have to quit my job. They were going to pay him $50.00 a week. We would have to find a place to live. It all seemed so big; it about scared us to death.

I remember we drove to the top of Fort Mountain, and went down a saw-mill road, and there he got on his knees in prayer and surrendered to the Lord to go to Mt. Olive. We found a house to rent in Rossville for $50.00 a month. We were only paying $20.00 a month for rent in Dalton. It all seemed so big to us, but we learned that if you have to do big things to please God, He always makes a way.

They were in a building program at Mt. Olive and trying to finish a new church. This was a new experience for Burman too. The deacons, building committee, and Burman were working together. They did a lot of the work themselves, and it didn't take long, and the money came right on in to finish the new auditorium. God was blessing the church with good services and people being saved and new members joining the church.

We just couldn't make it on $50.00 a week. So, I ended up with a job in Peerless Woolen Mills on third shift. This lasted about two years. The church was paid out of debt, so they gave Burman a raise in pay. The church bought a parsonage for us to live in. I got to give up my third shift job, and that was a happy day for me. We stayed at this church for six wonderful years. We could never forget about the great revival meetings we had and that we would have a week of prayer meetings each night before the revival. This would get everyone prayed up and ready for the meeting.

I guess one of the greatest revivals we had was when our son, Burman Jr., got saved. The night he was saved there were also ten or twelve boys and girls that were saved. I don't remember how many got saved that week, but it was a great meeting. Brother Ed Ballew was the evangelist. Brother Ed was always a good preacher to preach to the lost. Burman met Brother Ed right after he got saved. They were very good friends. They started preaching about the same time, I think.

There was something else we were excited about when we were at Mt. Olive. God blessed us with another eight-pound twelve-ounce baby boy, David Michael Cape. There are ten years difference between him and my first son, Junior.

Remember earlier in this book I wrote about when I got saved at nine years old. God was real in my life for a long while after I got saved. Then when I got old enough for the things of the world to be a temptation after Burman and I got married, I lost that joy that you have when you first get saved. I was so excited about Burman being saved and called to preach, but my personal relationship with God was not what it ought to be. You can't live and have victory yourself on somebody else's relationship. Really to be honest I was ashamed of what the Spirit of God did for me when I got saved, and I didn't want to act that way anymore. I was afraid of what people would think about me. God began to deal with my heart. We were having a revival at Mt. Olive, and everyone seemed happy but the pastor's wife. I even began to doubt my salvation.

66

One day when I was home by myself, I even tried to get saved again and that wouldn't work. I couldn't pray that sinner's prayer to save my life. No one knew, not even Burman, what was going on in my heart.

So, the revival closed, and I was still miserable. I knew deep in my heart I had to get willing to serve God like He wanted me to, regardless of what anyone thought. One day I bowed in the corner of my bedroom, and I told God I wanted that joy in my heart that only He could give. I told Him I would not be ashamed of old-time shouting and praising the Lord. I would do whatever He wanted me to do. God lifted that burden, and I felt so good; it seemed like the world had been lifted from my heart. When Sunday came again, God put me to the test. He had put a song in my heart to sing and a testimony. I was scared to death. My heart was beating so fast I felt like everybody in church could see it. God sent a blessing to my heart, and I've never forgotten it from that day. I've been hooked on obedience to Him because that is the only way to have peace.

God always has to break us before He can use us. We have to do things God's way and realize how weak we are but how strong God's power is. I could never be able to tell the joy I've had at home in my prayer time and with my Bible. His word and His promises come alive in my heart. Before I got the victory, I would only pray and read my Bible when I was in trouble, but when I got everything settled, God has made it my <u>daily bread</u>. I don't mean I've lived every day on the mountain top. There have been plenty of battles, storms, and trials to try my faith, but I just want to make it known that it's been worth every mile serving the Lord. Burman's ministry, our life together, our children, everything just had a new meaning to me.

We stayed at Mt. Olive Baptist Church for six years, then Burman believed that God was ready for him to leave. We left and went to Cloud Springs Baptist Church in Rossville, Georgia. We stayed there two years and had a good time but also a lot of storms and problems. There were a lot of good people there, but a lot of them were post-millennial, and Burman was pre-millennial. That really doesn't work too well together. I've heard Burman say that God put him there to teach him patience. In spite of it all we had a lot of people saved and always had a good crowd, and they were very good to us. I remember one Sunday night he preached to the lost and there were eighteen people saved. Pastor Brother Ronnie Childress was in that number, he was just a teen boy then.

Then at a time of discouragement (like the Devil always does), Calvary Baptist Church, Bridgeport, Alabama, called Burman. When you are discouraged, it is not a good time to make a decision. We left Cloud Springs, and he accepted Calvary Baptist. Did we ever get into trouble for this! We stayed there only seven months in a dry parched up land where no water was. I want to add this, Burman would say God whipped him for two years for leaving Cloud Springs Baptist Church at a time of discouragement.

Chapter 10

Bible Baptist Church

Burman stayed busy preaching revivals and Sundays for different churches. Then after a few months without a church some of the people from Rossville, Georgia, called him about starting Bible Baptist Church. After he had prayed about this, he believed this was what God wanted him to do. We started this church in a double car garage at one of the member's house. This was in February 1961. Some of these people he had pastored at Mt. Olive and a few from Cloud Springs. This was a big leap of faith to start a church from ground up. Burman and I and the charter members wanted a church to worship God in Spirit and in truth. The next big decision was where we would be located. It was not long until we needed more room. Then a couple of members, Brother Red and Mary Ruth Wilson owned some lots on Talley Lane just off of Happy Valley Road in Rossville, Georgia. They donated them for the purpose of building the church. The church is still located today at the same place. Brother and Sister Wilson have both gone on to be with the Lord.

Before long, we were able to build the basement of the church with Burman and some of the male members doing some of the work themselves. It was finished enough so we could have services. This was truly a great blessing. I remember they took the first offering for the building fund in a wheelbarrow. We stayed in the basement for about two years. Then they got the loan and built the auditorium and made Sunday School rooms in the basement.

We were having good services, and the attendance was growing. The first person to get saved lived next door to the church. I think she got under conviction while the basement was being built. Her name was Marie McAbee, and her husband, Paul, also got right. They made wonderful members. We had thirty-seven wonderful years at Bible Baptist Church. There is no way I could name all the great things God did for us. No, it was not all mountain top experiences. There have to be valleys between mountain tops. These are lessons of patience and faith. God blessed us with several souls saved. Several young men confessed their call to preach. Some of these men are still pastors today. Our son, Burman Jr., was one of the young men that confessed his call. Burman had our son to preach his first message the very night he confessed his call. It was called "Victory in Jesus." God has blessed him to be a pastor for over forty-three years. We thank God for this.

God blessed us to be able to support several missionaries and do a lot of home mission work. Bible Baptist Church was very good to us to support us and furnish us a nice car and a nice house to live in. While pastoring, Burman was able to preach revivals and was blessed in doing this. We were so blessed in his ministry at Bible Baptist. There were people who had babies and small children when we went there and some who were born after we went and grew up, got saved, finished school, got married and had children of their own. Many still go to Bible Baptist. We feel so blessed they are still our friends.

The last couple of years before we left was hard. Burman prayed so much about leaving because he remembered his experience of leaving Cloud Springs and how miserable we were. He wanted to be sure, so in December 1997 he got the answer, and we left in 1998. I think God kept us there until he got the next pastor prepared to take the church. Brother Ricky Gravley was finishing Faith Bible Institute. For us to leave was sad, but we were blessed in doing so, and the church was blessed because not one member left. We left in fellowship and loved everyone.

Chapter 11

Life After Pastoring

Now Burman said when God got through with him at Bible Baptist Church that he would leave and get out. He said I wouldn't be hanging around to torture the next pastor. At this time, we didn't even know Brother Gravley.

We had never thought we would leave our membership at Bible Baptist. When Burman wasn't preaching somewhere, we would visit different churches in our area. We just couldn't find a church home. Different pastors talked to us about joining their church, but it just didn't seem like the thing to do. In the meantime, we didn't go back to Bible Baptist for a year. We said that until we could find a church home we would send our tithes back to Bible Baptist, and that's what we did.

We met Brother Gravley and his family, and it was like we had been friends forever. We went back for Homecoming, and it was great. God met with us, and the members gave us a great welcome. Brother Gravley and Burman talked, and Brother Gravley was gracious to us and welcomed us just to leave our membership at Bible Baptist. Brother Gravley has told us that God showed him that if he would be good to that preacher (Burman), that God would be good to him and bless him. When we would go back, it was just to have a church home and a place to worship God. We didn't have any voice with anyone about anything in the church because we knew that was Brother Gravley's job, and it worked out perfect. We could feel at home to enjoy the services. Our son David is the choir director at Bible Baptist Church at this present time. What a blessing to our hearts.

From 1998 until 2010, Burman was blessed by God to have a place to preach almost every Sunday and Sunday night. He also preached revivals until he was diagnosed with cancer in 2006. He had to start cutting the meetings back, but he went on Sundays until October 4, 2010, which was his last service he preached.

We had no idea when he would quit preaching. His heart's desire was to preach until he died. But on his death bed, when he was able to pray, he would beg God to touch his body and let him preach again. As long as he was conscious, he still wanted to preach.

I have so many good memories of these twelve years. We traveled to so many good churches. The pastors that invited us to come, we loved them so much. God took care of us in so many ways. He supplied everything we ever needed. I prayed so much about our safety on the road. God so graciously answered prayer.

I just wanted to tell you some of the things God did for us! The thing is, God still saves today. If you will call upon His name, He will make a wonderful change in your life!

Chapter 12

Amazing Things God Did

There was a revival we were going to in South Carolina. We left on Saturday and were in Dalton, Georgia, when suddenly our car caught on fire. Burman pulled off the road, and we got out of the car. Traffic stopped; people got out to see if they could help. No one had fire extinguishers to put out the fire. We got our clothes out of the car. Someone had called the fire department, but our car would have been burned up before they came. Suddenly a Frito Lay Truck stopped. My nephew, Jim Roach was the driver, and he had a fire extinguisher. He put out the fire with not too much damage. The car was not drivable, but it was able to be repaired. Now the strange thing, Jim was not even supposed to be working on Saturday and had decided he would just go ahead and run this route for one of his employees. You see, God had him at the right place at the right time with just what we needed. We had to cancel the meeting in South Carolina.

We had the car towed to Queen's Auto Shop in Ringgold, Georgia. Mr. Queen always did our work on our car, and in a few days, the car was running again. You couldn't tell anything had happened to the car, but this is the kind of work Mr. Queen did. But the big surprise was when Burman got out the checkbook to pay him, and of course, we had no idea how much it would cost, and Mr. Queen said there was no charge. He said God had put it on his heart to not charge anything. Can you believe how God takes care of His children!

Then another time when we were going out of town on a trip, we had to do some shopping in Fort Oglethorpe. We got out of our car and went into the store, came back and our car would not start. When it was checked out the battery was dead. The strange thing was we were in the parking lot in front of the Auto Zone. We purchased a battery from there and drove on home.

Another time, we came home from a long trip and our car broke down in our driveway. It just wouldn't start, and we had to have some work done on the car. But the thing is, it didn't break down until we got all the way home. God was so good to us. We could have been stranded on the road.

One time when God took care of us, he had preached for Brother Tony Hudson in Murfreesboro, Tennessee. Brother Tony, as he always did, begged us to stay all night and not drive home late at night. Burman was determined he was going home and sleep in his bed. It was a cold night; we came across Monteagle Mountain, and God so graciously let us get home safe. The next morning Burman and our son David were going somewhere. David pulled the car out of our garage and all the anti-freeze had leaked out. The radiator had burst. The hand of God was with us. It could have happened on the way home, but God was watching out for us. Just like He always did!

Chapter 13

An Appreciation for God's Blessings!

I don't really know the words or how to explain how much I appreciate all the pastors and churches for all they did for us. We met so many good friends and had a wonderful time the twelve years he was in evangelistic work. We enjoyed every day of it. Although we still missed the churches he pastored too. We knew we were blessed beyond measure. One of my biggest regrets is that I didn't write down all of his meetings, revivals, weddings, funerals, and every special event. But most of all I wished I had written the people's names down who got saved and baptized. It would be wonderful to have that!

Writing this book has filled a lot of lonely hours for me. I can't explain the emptiness in my heart with him gone. Life can never be the same. I thank God for sixty-six wonderful blessed years we had together.

God has taken care of me in so many ways. When we got the word that Burman had cancer, I knew the time would probably come, and it would take his life. I prayed to God that He would just give me the strength to stay by his side. God granted me that prayer, and I praise His name!